Jonathan Holmes

Katrina

A Play of New Orleans

Published by Methuen Drama 2009

1 3 5 7 9 10 8 6 4 2

Methuen Drama
A & C Black Publishers Limited
36 Soho Square
London W1D 3QY
www.methuendrama.com

ISBN 978 1 408 12549 6

A CIP catalogue record for this book is available from
the British Library

Typeset by Country Setting, Kingsdown, Kent CT14 8ES
Printed and bound in Great Britain by
CPI Cox & Wyman, Reading, RG1 8EX

This book is produced using paper that is made from wood grown in managed, sustainable forests. It is natural, renewable and recyclable. The logging and manufacturing processes conform to the environmental regulations of the country of origin.

Jericho House

presents

Katrina

A Play of New Orleans

by Jonathan Holmes

First performed on 1 September 2009
at The Bargehouse, Oxo Tower Wharf

Funded by

The Brook Trust

Katrina

By Jonathan Holmes

Cast

Beatrice	Andrea Harris
Miranda	Wunmi Mosaku
Dan	Joe Speare
Cal	Andrew Dennis
Lorrie	Stephanie Langton
Larry	Orlando Wells
Musician	Michael Mwenso
Additional voice cast	John Hurt, Emma North

Crew

Director	Jonathan Holmes
Producers	Suzanne Cristinacce (for Jericho House) Jonathan Holmes
Designer	Lucy Wilkinson
Composer	Peter Readman
Sound Designer	Peter Nash (for Monty Funk)
Lighting Designer	Paul J. Need (for 10 out of 10)
Assistant Director	Ilana Winterstein
Production Manager	Ellen Mainwood
Video Designer	Nick Price
Press	Janine Shalom, Amy Barder (for Premier)
Marketing	Nicci Alt, Christine Pillainayagam (for TargetLive)
Assistant Designers	Olivia Altaras (sculpture) Christopher Gylee (costume) Lauren Nikrooz
Stage Manager	Aaron Minnigen
Deputy Stage Manager	Jennifer Simpson
Assistant Stage Manager	Naomi Buchanan Brooks
House Manager	Ilana Winterstein
Chief Electrician	Ken Coker (for 10 out of 10)
Assistant Electrician	Rhys West (for 10 out of 10)
Technician	Jonathan Monkhouse
Design Team	Ben Austin, Helen Coyston, Kate Matthews, Eunyoung Sung, Kate Theodore, Joanne Tweedle, Elizabeth Vicary, Stephanie Williams
Website Designers	Nick Price, Lucy Wilkinson

Voice Coaches	Tim Charrington, Yvonne Morley
Poster and Leaflet Designer	Lucy Wilkinson
Foyer Designers	Alice Bray, Joe Fairweather Hole
Photographer	Thierry Bal
Researcher	Marianne Le Gallo
Box Office	Chris Campbell & team at the Young Vic
Equipment Hire	10 out of 10 Productions

Acknowledgements

Our sincere gratitude to the New Orleanians who gave their time and testimony to this project, to all those in the US and elsewhere who encouraged and assisted with our work, and most of all to the six individuals who allowed their remarkable stories to be re-told as theatre.

Sections of this play use the words of Larry Bradshaw and Lorrie Beth Slonsky from their article in Socialist Worker newspaper (US), "The real heroes and sheroes of New Orleans," September 9, 2005 (http://socialistworker.org/2005-2/556/556_04_RealHeroes.shtml).

Thanks to Lola Vollen, Chris Ying and Dave Eggers for permission to use extracts from their book *Voices from the Storm*, a volume in the 'Voice of Witness' series.

The Jericho House wishes to thank the following, for all their help in enabling *Katrina* to happen:

Rebekah Caudwell, Sarah Jones, John Hurt, Lillian Boutte, Jean Toussaint, David Morrison, Matilda Leyser, David Lan, Chris Campbell and all at the Young Vic, Phil Evans and all at the Pleasance, Tony Greenwood, Yamaha, Professor Sophie Scott and ICN, Steve Cross, Abbas Nokhasteh, Chipo Chung, George Fenton, The New Orleans Tourist Office, Steve, Janet and all at the 606 Club, Cristina Fernandez, Anthony Arnove, Nadeem Azhar, Emma North, Sasha Roberts, Rose McAfee, Antonia Christophers, Shereen Martineau, Jenny Sweet, Gayle Lawson, Chipping Norton theatre, Stephanie De Howes, Coin St Community Builders, Peter Holland, Romana Huk, Phelim & friends at D & D, Keith Steadman.

Such a large production could not have been realised without the help of a number of dedicated volunteers and ushers, most of whom came on board after this programme went to press and so sadly cannot be credited here. We wish to thank them all for their generous support and their time.

A very special thanks must be reserved for Tim Bull and Rosalind Riley, remarkable friends without whom this production would never have been possible.

The Jericho House specialises in groundbreaking alliances between theatre, music and installation art. Our principal focus is on the undervalued world of sound, and our themes are hospitality, refuge and the city.

The Jericho House is more than just a company; we are a nomadic venue. We are invited to occupy buildings, whether theatres, galleries or abandoned structures, and we in turn invite others to join us in our experiments. We then collaborate with visionary partners to create idealistic and supple performance environments for the staging of dynamic, ethical work.

The principal aims of **The Jericho House** are:

- To create exciting and radical new performance works.
- To find new languages for theatre.
- To make work with an ethical, transformative purpose.
- To produce work that engages with the disenfranchised within communities.
- To foster relationships with dynamic collaborators, wherever we may find them, across all media.
- To develop work that improves the breadth and depth of knowledge about topics of concern in the world.
- To cultivate alliances concerning fundamental aspects of theatrical representation: perception, the body, space, and narrative experience.
- To restore to theatre its central place in the cultural, creative and intellectual life of society.

The Jericho House was founded by Jonathan Holmes

www.jerichohouse.org.uk

Jericho House Company Biographies

Suzanne Cristinacce (producer)

Suzanne Cristinacce is a producer and joined **The Jericho House** in 2008. *Katrina* is her first major production. Prior to becoming a producer she studied Russian and German at the University of Bristol. This led to international development work in Russia, Mongolia and Mauritius, where she advised on NGO management and helped set up local volunteering schemes. She has also worked for several years within the community care sector with homeless people and drug users in Cambridge, Lambeth and Hackney, focusing on client participation in the running of support services. She has an MSc in Drug Use: Evidence-Based Policy and Intervention from Imperial College, London.

Andrew Dennis (Cal)

Andrew Dennis trained at Mountview Theatre School.

Theatre credits include: *As You Like It* (Curve Theatre, Leicester), *The Full Monty* (Key Theatre, Peterborough), *Don Quixote* (West Yorkshire and Theatre Madrid), *Three Sisters* (Birmingham Rep and UK Tour), *Othello* (US Tour), *Jeff Koons* (ATC UK Tour), *Wonderful Town* (Grange Park Opera), *Bouncers* (West End and UK Tour), *Tales From Ovid, A Midsummer Night's Dream* and *Timon From Athens* (RSC), *BlueBird* (Royal Court) and Cailban in *Une Tempete.*

Television credits include: *Doctors, Down To Earth, Dream Team, Red Cap, My Hero, Jeffery Archer – The Truth, Surprising Stars, The Bill, Hale and Pace, and Shelley.*

Film credits include: *Mothers and Daughters* and *Rhythm and Blue.*

Andrea Harris (Beatrice)

Andrea Harris trained at the Bristol Old Vic and the American Conservatory Theatre.

Recent theatre credits include: Titania in *A Midsummer Night's Dream* at Stratford-upon-Avon and in the West End for the RSC.

Also for the RSC: *Hamlet* and *Love's Labours' Lost* (2008-9 Stratford/London season). Other theatre includes: *To Kill a Mockingbird* (Birmingham Rep, West Yorkshire Playhouse and UK Tour), *A Streetcar Named Desire* (Theatr Clywd), *The Resurrection of Roscoe Powell* (Soho Theatre), *New Lives* (Scarlett Theatre), *A Midsummer Night's Dream* (Les Blancs, Pericles, Chicago, Oregon Shakespeare Festival), *Mules* (Magic Theatre, San Francisco), *Blues for an Alabama Sky* (Theatreworks, San Francisco – Critics Circle Award).

Television credits include: *Hamlet* (RSC/BBC), *Dr Who, Doctors, Casualty, Make Way For Noddy, My Hero.*

Film credits include: *Last Chance Harvey, True Story.*

Radio credits include: *Passing, Gunpoint Optimism, Ah, Wilderness!, Each Day Dies With Sleep, Melancholy Baby.*

Jonathan Holmes (writer/director/producer)

Dr. Jonathan Holmes is a director, playwright, scholar, and founder of **The Jericho House**. For the company he wrote, directed and produced *Fallujah* on Brick Lane in 2007, with a score by Nitin Sawhney and design by Lucy Orta. A book about the play was published the same year. He has since directed *Orpheus Behind the Wire* (Bond/Henze) and *Figure Humaine* (Poulenc/Eluard) as a collaboration with Harry Christophers and The Sixteen at the South Bank Centre, and has written the libretto (a translation from Hafiz), for Liza Lim's new opera *Tongue of the Invisible*. In 2005 he premiered unheard songs by John Donne at St Paul's Cathedral, where they were performed by Dame Emma Kirkby, Carolyn Sampson and others. As a scholar he has written extensively on Donne, Shakespeare and the philosophy of aesthetics, publishing two books on these subjects, *Merely Players?* and *Refiguring Mimesis*, in 2004 and 2005. His feature film *Perpetual Peace*, about global grassroots conflict resolution, will be released in 2010. He was once Senior Lecturer in Drama at Royal Holloway, where he set up a new English-Drama degree, and has otherwise directed fifteen other theatre productions (many of them site-specific) and written articles for numerous publications over the years, including *Modern Poetry in Translation, Shakespeare Survey* and *The Guardian*. www.jonathanholmes.net.

Stephanie Langton (Lorrie)

Theatre credits include: Aaron Sorkin's *A Few Good Men*, Sir Richard Eyre's production of *Hedda Gabler* and *The Things Good Men Do* (Lyric Hammersmith), *Fool for Love, Closer, Comedy of Errors, The Country* (Belgrade Theatre, Coventry).

Television credits include: female lead in the forthcoming TV drama *Werewolves* (Discovery/ITV Global), the Bafta winning *The Government Inspector* (Channel 4), *Jekyll* (BBC), *Holby Blue*.

She took her first leading role on film in the Hong Kong/UK action movie *Bodyguard: A New Beginning*, released in 2009.

Ellen Mainwood (production manager)

Ellen Mainwood is a production manager, and this is her second production working for **The Jericho House**. She studied Theatre at Royal Holloway before working in marketing at The Marlowe Theatre, Canterbury and in education at Chipping Norton Theatre. She was producer and production manager on Jonathan Holmes' previous project, *Fallujah*, and is delighted to be working with the company again on *Katrina*.

Wunmi Mosaku (Miranda)

Wunmi Mosaku trained at RADA.

Theatre credits include: *Mules* (Young Vic), *The Vertical Hour* (Royal Court), *Rough Crossings* (Headlong Tour and Lyric Hammersmith), *The Great Theatre of the World* (Arcola Theatre).

Television credits include: *One Night In Emergency* (BBC), *Silent Witness* (BBC), *Father and Son* (Leftbank Pics/ITV), *Moses Jones* (BBC 2), *The Clinic* (RTE/Elixir TV), *The Bill* (ITV), *Never Better* (World Prods/BBC 2), *Sold* (ITV), *Weirdos* (Rough Cut/BBC 3).

She recently finished work on her first feature film, *Womb* (Razor Film Produktion).

Michael Mwenso (musician)

Michael Mwenso is a singer, trombonist, organist and all round musician who has been playing music since an early age.

He began playing with the Rock n Roll group 'Jive Aces' when he was very young, touring European music festivals and performing with clarinetist Acker Bilk. Aged 12 he was invited to perform with the James Brown Show during James Brown's UK tours. He has played with JB Horns Maceo Parker, Fred Wesley and Pee Wee Ellis (Jazz Café and Shepherds Bush Empire), Gary Crosby, Jazz Jamaica All Stars, and was the featured trombonist on trumpeter Abram Wilson's BBC Jazz award nominated album 'Ride Ferris Wheel to the Modern Delta'. He was part of the Dune Music Tribute Series (Spice of Life), and in 2008 he opened the London Jazz Festival at the Royal Albert Hall. He ran a series of events called 'Side by Side' at Ronnie Scott's during the Jazz festival, and he currently has a resident spot at Ronnie Scott's running a Wednesday night Jam session which has received international acclaim.

Peter Nash (sound designer)

Peter Nash is a sound designer and creative director at Monty Funk Productions. Since the mid-nineties, Pete's background has been in sound design and technical presentation for radio broadcast and theatrical audiences. As independent suppliers to BBC Radio 4 and BBC Radio 3, his work can be heard in many cutting-edge drama/documentary works, including Radio 3's 'Between The Ears' experimental audio strand. He specialises in soundscape design for challenging environments, such as site-specific theatre. Pete has been working with **The Jericho House** on the soundscapes for *Katrina* since November 2008.

Paul J. Need (lighting designer)

Paul Need is a lighting designer who trained at The Royal Academy of Dramatic Art, where he later joined the staff teaching lighting design and stage electrics. He has been a lighting designer since 1980 and has now officially lost count of how many productions he has lit in theatre, dance, opera and music. This is his second production for **The Jericho House**, having previously designed for *Fallujah*. He has also worked as a sound engineer, production manager, production electrician and chief electrician (Sadler's Wells Opera). Credits include *La Bohème*, (Scottish Opera); Syria's first opera production *Dido & Aeneas* (staged in a number of Roman Amphitheatres); *The Wasteland* (Donmar Warehouse) and the British Premier of John Adams' *I was looking at the ceiling and saw the sky* (Royal Opera House, Linbury). *Hérodiade, Turandot & The Pearl Fishers* (Dorset Opera), and for many opera companies such as: Traveling Opera, Crystal Clear Opera, Opera Viva, Music Theatre Kernow, Modern Music Theatre Troupe, Minatuar Opera, New Sussex Opera, Surrey Opera, Mid-Wales Opera, British Youth Opera, Snape Maltings, East End Opera, Opera East, Holland Park, Bloomsbury Opera, Armonico Consort & Guildford Opera. He is also a freelance photographer, General Manager of Co-Opera Co and Managing Director of 10 out of 10 Productions.

Peter Readman (composer)

Peter Readman is a composer and musical director. He has been performing, directing and composing jazz, theatre and concert music for most of his life. Credits include composing the musical scores for *The Dream Snatcher* (2008, Haberdashers' Federation), *Sadly Solo Joe* (Greenwich theatre 2003), *Hooker!* (2005), as well as numerous vocal compositions, among them settings of John Donne poems, 'The Triple Fool' and 'The Message' premiered by Harry Christophers and The Sixteen (St Paul's Cathedral 2007). Other works include 'Fractal Fugues for piano' (2008-09), 'Crystals' for Harp and Chamber Orchestra. His work as a musical director includes *Sweeney Agonistes* and *The Mystery Plays* (Bath Festival 2007-2009), *Fallujah* (Jonathan Holmes, 2007) and *A Christmas Carol* (for Anvil Arts, Basingstoke, 2008). He is also composer-in-residence at Haberdashers' Askes Hatcham College in South London, and teaches composition and musicianship at Centre for Young Musicians, as well as giving workshops in music composition throughout the UK.

Joe Speare (Dan)

Theatre credits include: *The Harder They Come* (The Barbican, Birmingham and West End), *Carmen Jones* (Southbank), *The King And I* (Irish tour), *Boogie Nights* (national and South African tour), *The Official Tribute To The Blues Brothers* (national and international tours), *Smokey Joe's Cafe* (national tour), *To Kill A Mockingbird* (Birmingham Rep, West Yorkshire Playhouse and National Tour), *Harvey, Nude With Violin* (Royal Exchange), *The Mysteries 2003, Twelfth Night, Of Mice and Men, Martin Chuzzlewit, Bouncers, The Tokolosh* (Belgrade, Coventry), *The Revenger's Tragedy* (West Yorkshire Playhouse), *Peter Pan, Toad of Toad Hall* (Birmingham Rep), *Waiting For Godot, The Double, Man Friday* (Liverpool Playhouse).

Television and film credits include: *Prime Suspect, Cracker, Coronation Street, Children's Ward* (Granada), *Raffle Baby* (Real Life Productions), *Emmerdale* (Yorkshire), *The Bill* (Thames), *That Peter Kay Thing* (Open Mike Productions), *Cold Earth* (Gatlin Pictures).

Radio credits include: *September Song, The Last of The Mohicans, Anacaona* (BBC Radio 4).

Orlando Wells (Larry)

Theatre credits include: *Our Country's Good* at The Watermill Theatre, *The History Boys* at the National Theatre, Prandello's *Henry IV* at the Donmar Warehouse, *A Midsummer Night's Dream* and *The Modernists* at the Sheffield Crucible Theatre, *A Midsummer Night's Dream* for the Royal Shakespeare Company and *Shakespeare in the Dark* at the BAC.

Television credits include *Doctors, Holby City, The Bill* and *As If* for Channel 4.

Lucy Wilkinson (designer)

Lucy Wilkinson MA holds degrees in Illustration/Animation (Manchester School of Art), and in English Literature (Oxford University), and a Postgraduate Diploma in Theatre Design from Bristol Old Vic Theatre School. In 2005 her design work was short-listed for the Linbury Biennial Prize for Stage Design and the Jocelyn Herbert Award for Stage Design. Design credits include *Fallujah* (Old Truman Brewery, costume design), *Frozen* (Riverside Studios and touring); *Company, Chook Chook* (Bristol Old Vic); *A Small Family Business, The Marriage of Figaro* (Redgrave Theatre, Bristol); *The Marriage of Figaro* (Warwick Arts Centre/touring); *Iolanthe* (Minack Theatre); *Much Ado About Nothing* (RSC Swan, educational tour); *Taming of the Shrew* (Guildford Shakespeare Company); sets at the National Film School; *Larkrise* and *Candleford* (Oxford School of Drama); *The Passion of Christ, Tales from the Brothers Grimm, Measure for Measure* (Creation Theatre); *Arabian Nights, Trelawney of the Wells* (Colchester Mercury). Assistant design credits include *The Wizard of Oz, Carmen Jones* (Royal Festival Hall); *Merchant of Venice* (Galaxy Theatre, Tokyo); *The Tempest* (Tara Arts); *Journey's End, Wedding Day at the Cro-Magnons* (Colchester Mercury). Lucy also illustrates fiction and poetry for all ages, and creates the graphic artwork for production posters. She regularly designs the cover for the international poetry magazine *Modern Poetry in Translation.*

Ilana Winterstein (assistant director)

Ilana Winterstein is a theatre practitioner who trained at the Central School of Speech and Drama, achieving a Masters degree in Performing, as well as a BA Hons degree in English Literature (Birmingham University). She specialises in devised and physical theatre, and is also a writer and director. Since graduating CSSD she has worked with Conflict Zone Arts Asylum in Berlin, been a member of the Soho Theatre Young Writers Group, created work at Shunt as part of the NetAudio Festival, is an experienced theatre workshop leader, and has performed in various theatre productions and short films.

Theatre and Experience

by Jonathan Holmes

'To try to understand the experience of another it is necessary to dismantle the world as seen from one's place within it, and to reassemble it as seen from his . . . To talk of entering the other's subjectivity is misleading. The subjectivity of another does not simply constitute a different interior attitude to the same exterior facts. *The constellation of facts, of which he is the centre, is different.*'

John Berger, *A Seventh Man*

In theatre, as in life, events are always observed from somewhere. There is always a point of view, changing constantly – like life, theatre happens in more than two dimensions. It is the only medium with the capacity wholly to surround its audience with tangible reality, and it is the sole artform with the ability to create, as well as to represent, live experience.

To understand the world we need to comprehend the exterior as well as the interior structures of experience. Theatre's great advantage over other media is that it has the potential to do this effortlessly. It can create exterior 'constellations of facts', in Berger's words, and it can depict the ways in which they transform or influence individual subjectivities. Other artforms cannot achieve this as readily, for the simple reason that they have not the capacity to sculpt four-dimensional space. The potency of theatre lies in this ability both to represent experience and to create it in the bodies and minds of all those present. It not only portrays change, it enacts it.

Theatre is able to dismantle one world and assemble another, both metaphorically and actually, all around us. The role of theatrical space is consequently not just scenic, but essentially political. In reality our experience of the world is primarily a sensory one; not only visual but also aural, tactile, olefactory. So it can be in theatre. In reality we react to space bodily – we are moved in a physical as well as in an intellectual or an emotional sense. Why not too in the theatre? Crucially, such a conceptual and spatial reconfiguration in how theatre works is not in service of a new naturalism, where the focus is on representation, but rather attends to the actual experience of those present – that of the storytellers, certainly, but most centrally that of the audience.

This kind of theatre does not supplant genuine experience, replacing it with the virtual; it *is* experience, of the same order and dimension as everyday life. We are all in the room together, manufacturing memories; why not be honest about it? The role of such theatre is not conspiratorially to pretend that an illusion is real (the job rather of politicians and priests), but to acknowledge that we are all sharing an actual, and possibly profound, experience together. There are no illusions, only experiences. This theatre is a kind of cubist artform, presenting simultaneously the many sides of experience, though it goes beyond anything painting can achieve by welcoming within itself the experiences of its audience, too. The audience is the subject of the performance as much as the narrative or the characters, and as central a participant as the actors or the crew. We do not need to be in a specially sanctified building for all this to obtain; it can happen more or less anywhere. After all, theatre is really a kind of refuge, not a market; it is naturally hospitable, not mercantile.

A consequence of all this is a re-imagining of the role of the audience. It ceases to be a band of consumers, paying for the familiar, and becomes instead a collective of witnesses, vital to the event's integrity. Such a shift is partly ethical in nature, as auditors and spectators are free to choose how closely they engage with the material and how involved they become in the unfolding events. This is clearest when testimony is at the heart of the experience, as in *Katrina*, and the audience is witness to a form of public hearing of untold stories. The responses the stories engender are vital to their meaning, and the audience, by its presence, is a kind of collaborator in their authorship.

The function of any narrative is to make experience recognisable. Stories are the necessary means by which the oppressed articulate their oppression, and by which the abused seek to heal their wounds. They are the starting point for understanding, for awareness, and for empathy. They can be a vehicle for the transmission of joy. The shape that an individual storyteller gives to their experience can make us see the familiar afresh, make us see a situation as if for the first time. Stories, famously, make the stone stony – the opposite of an anaesthetic is the aesthetic.

A theatrical emphasis on experience, then, points in two directions. As an act itself, attending a performance is experiential, we are a part of that event, part of the story, immersed in its sensual space and sharing responsibility for its occurrence. And as a representation, theatre serves to make the experience of others recognisable according to certain perceptual and cultural codes. The combination of the two means that as audience members our attention is directed many ways – inward into ourselves, across to our fellow witnesses, outside the building and into the world, and often into the past, too. It follows that such a theatrical experience shatters boundaries between several parallel incarnations of 'us' and 'them', of the powerful and the powerless. It is both empathetic and egalitarian, and so profoundly ethical.

It is in the counterpoint of these understandings, the sensory and the perceptual, that the potency of theatrical aesthetics resides. The more the body is engaged on its own terms with the work, the more those attending are involved, implicated and affected by the experience, and so the further any ethical potential is developed. In its emphasis on the sensory and the experiential, this kind of theatre prioritises the perception of individual bodies as ends in themselves and not as a means to some further representation. This is evident in the fact that, unlike much consumer-theatre, this kind of performance cannot exist without an audience present. Our theatre is an art of solidarity, not of division.

Such a simple reconfiguration of a medium as this has significant and radical implications. In a fully enveloping, four-dimensional space, the opportunities open to playwrights, designers, directors and performers expand and deepen almost beyond measure – literally as well as figuratively. The complexity and relevance such a change endows also restores to theatre a uniqueness and a seriousness that in our crowded culture had come close to being crushed. Most of all, though, it foregrounds the ethical authority of the artform, reviving its ancient function as a mouthpiece of resistance and place of change, not just rhetorical but actual. The natural role of theatre is the transformation of lives.

Katrina

Hurricane Katrina and New Orleans

Hurricane Katrina, weakening from a Category 5 to a Category 4 storm, struck the Louisiana coast on 29 August 2005. It veered east of the city of New Orleans, striking Lake Pontchartrain and causing sizeable surges across its twenty-five-mile surface. The defensive levees protecting the city from the lake, which had been left in disrepair for decades, were swiftly overcome, and eventually 80 per cent of the city was flooded. At the same time the Mississippi burst its banks, leading to all but a handful of viable exits from New Orleans being submerged.

The Mayor had ordered a mandatory evacuation of the city several hours earlier, but in a city of a million souls there was not the time, and most of the poorest had not the capability, for this to be effectively realised. Over 100,000 people were either trapped or chose to remain in the city as a result. For the next week, despite the presence of the world's media, the US government spectacularly failed to deliver aid to the waterlogged city, and in many cases the pedestrian evacuation of residents was actively prevented by local law enforcement, while the Federal Emergency Management Agency turned away rescue teams trying to enter the city.

Approximately twelve people died during the hurricane itself, whereas in contrast almost two thousand perished in the ensuing week of inactivity. The final infrastructural cost is estimated at $100 billion. By September 2005, 85 per cent of the population of New Orleans was officially displaced from the city. In September 2006 the authorities were still recovering bodies from flattened houses, and by September 2009 many residents, especially in the poorest areas, had yet to be allowed back into their homes and had received neither insurance payouts nor compensation. In the combination of loss of life and loss of livelihood and infrastructure, the failure to rescue New Orleans constitutes the largest disaster ever to occur on US soil.

Synopsis of the Play

Virgil, a decadent old New Orleanian, dies during Hurricane Katrina. Trapped by the rising flood water, his partner Beatrice determines to take his body to safety at City Hall. During her journey she encounters a number of other survivors and hears their stories.

Staging

The design should reflect the ruinous and sodden state of the city after the flood. The principal staging conceit is taken from the New Orleans predilection for processions, whether Mardi Gras carnivals, Easter parades, jazz funerals or roaming zygot bands, themselves echoes of the migrant journeys that led to such a heterogeneous cultural base. Aspects of all of these are encoded in the text, and should be echoed in the design.

Sound

The most important element of the play, aside from the testimonies themselves, is the one most tricky to script. There should be a continuous, integrated, complex soundscape-cum-score running throughout. Although at times song is called for, the aural landscape should not be that of operetta or musical, and nor should it always underscore action in a conventional sense. Rather it is conceived that there be a parallel and contrapuntal auditory language, freighted with thematic and narrative meaning, enhancing and departing from the visual and textual narratives as appropriate.

Testimony

Some of Beatrice's testimony has been adjusted. Everything spoken by any other character is entirely verbatim, and garnered from interviews and accounts written by those concerned.

Characters

NEW ORLEANIANS

Beatrice
Miranda
Daniel
Cal
Virgil, *deceased*
A Preacher

TRAPPED VISITORS

Larry Robinson
Lorrie Robinson

Authentic archive voices of various journalists, politicians and survivors

The playscript that follows was correct at time of going to press, but may have changed during rehearsal.

Reflecting the play's first site-specific performance by The Jericho House at The Bargehouse in London, the play is divided into 'storeys' rather than 'scenes'. For subsequent incarnations in other spaces these terms can naturally be removed, though it may be handy to retain the broad structural transitions they implicitly mark.

Storey One

The audience arrives at the venue and is told to wait outside until the stroke of eight p.m. Auditors are given disposable rain coverings, such as Americans wear in Scotland, though these should be black rather than the usual transparent plastic. As they enter the building they ascend a staircase, the sides of which are recognisable as corroded and groaning levee walls. At the top of the stairs they then go into the first of many rooms, the threshold of which is capped with horn.

INTRO

The first room is a tourist information office. Maps and pictures line the walls, and a TV plays a 'Come to New Orleans' video on loop. The office should be sincere, not parodic, and provide genuine contextual information about the city, though in the circumstances the commercialism will of course appear glib.

Over the PA the following text quietly plays:

> And it came to pass after seven days that the waters of the flood were upon the earth. The same day were all the fountains of the great deep broken up, and the windows of heaven were opened. And the rain was upon the earth forty days and forty nights. The waters prevailed exceedingly upon the earth; and all the high hills, that were under the whole heaven, were covered. Fifteen cubits upward did the waters prevail; and the mountains were covered. All flesh died that moved upon the earth, both of fowl, and of cattle, and of beast, and of every creeping thing that creepeth upon the earth, and every man. And the waters prevailed upon the earth a hundred and fifty days.
>
> And God made a wind to pass over the earth, and the waters assuaged. The fountains also of the deep and the windows of heaven were stopped, and the rain from

heaven was restrained. And the waters returned from off the earth continually: and after the end of the hundred and fifty days the waters were abated. The waters decreased continually until the ninth month: in the ninth month, on the first day of the month, were the tops of the mountains seen.

Storey Two

FUNKY BUTT

At the far end of the tourist office another staircase leads further upwards; again there is the sense of creaking levees on either side. On the second floor the environment opens out somewhat, and the spaces are less claustrophobic. The audience moves at its own pace through a 'shotgun' house, belonging to an absent New Orleanian family, and then an adjacent bar, 'The Funky Butt'. Here the audience meets some of the characters who speak later, and who are either employed by or visiting the bar: **Miranda** *may sing, and some of the others hang out, drinking. A musician, a pianist, encourages some audience members to sit; he will subsequently follow the action around the building and accompany the cast on a sequence of instruments, including a trombone. The following announcements are heard in ever-louder loops, while TVs in the house and the bar show meteorological maps and imagery of the hurricane:*

National Weather Service Warning
(*1 a.m., Sunday 28 August 2005*)
Hurricane Katrina, a most powerful hurricane with unprecedented strength . . . Devastating damage expected . . . Most of the area will be uninhabitable for weeks, perhaps longer. At least half of well-constructed homes will have roof and wall failure. All gabled roofs will fail, leaving those homes severely damaged or destroyed. The majority of industrial buildings will become non-functional. Partial to complete wall and roof failure is expected. All wood framed low-rising apartment buildings will be destroyed. Concrete-block low-rise apartment buildings will sustain major damage, including some wall and roof failure. High-rise office and apartment buildings will sway dangerously, a few to the point of total collapse. All windows will blow out. Airborne debris will be widespread, and may include heavy items such as household appliances and even light vehicles. Sport utility vehicles and light trucks will be moved. The blown debris will create additional destructions.

Persons, pets and livestock exposed to the winds will face certain death if struck. Power outages will last for weeks, as most power poles will be down and transformers destroyed. Water shortages will make human suffering incredible by modern standards. The vast majority of native trees will be snapped or uprooted, only the heartiest will remain standing. Livestock exposed to the winds will be killed.

There is a pause. Then:

Governor Kathleen Blanco

I have determined that this incident is of such severity and magnitude that effective response is beyond the capabilities of the State and affected local governments, and that supplementary Federal assistance is necessary to save lives, protect property, public health and safety, or to lessen or avert the threat of a disaster.

The shelters will end up probably without electricity or with minimum electricity from generators in the end. There may be intense flooding that will be not in our control which would be ultimately the most dangerous situation that many of our people could face.

But I believe we are prepared. That's the one thing that I've always been able to brag about.

Mayor Ray Nagin

A mandatory evacuation order is hereby called for all of the parish of Orleans. We are facing a storm that most of us have feared. I don't want to create panic, but I do want the citizens to understand that this is very serious, and it is of the highest nature.

The loop builds in intensity and we are able now to hear the beginning of the hurricane. Gradually the storm noise increases until it drowns the text, at which point there is an electrical explosion and all lights and visuals go off. In the darkness the noise of the storm is huge, and wind now is felt, strong and insistent. This continues for three or four minutes before subsiding.

Storey Three

PART ONE: MAIN SPACE

Having been encouraged to leave the 'flooding' bar, the audience is now shepherded up the stairs, via emergency lighting, to the next floor. The stairwell is graffitied: 'Abandon hope all ye who enter'; 'FEMA evacuation strategy: run, motherfucker, run!'' etc. This floor is to be the principal performance space. In appearance it should be recognisable as 'The Funky Butt' once again, but now wrecked by wind and water. More graffiti and other symbols are emblazoned on the walls, including the 'X' hieroglyphs indicating that a derelict house has been searched and communicating what was found within. The wall at the rear of the bar has been breached, allowing us to see into another ruined building, which is revealed as a storehouse for Mardi Gras equipment. At the rear of this is a large carnival float, now mildewed and damaged by the storm, surrounded by large masks and other paraphernalia.

The testimony in this section is reproduced wherever possible from authentic recordings and is heard, overlapping, on the PA only. The space remains in near-total darkness throughout.

Mayor Ray Nagin
We come to you with facts. We come to you with eye-witness accounts. We come to you because we were there before the storm hit, we were there when the storm hit, we were there after the storm, and we're still there . . .

BBC Journalist
A large section of the vital 17th Street Canal levee, where it connects to the brand new 'hurricane-proof' Old Hammond Highway Bridge, gave way late Monday morning in Bucktown after Katrina's fiercest winds were well north. The breach sent a churning sea of water from Lake Pontchartrain coursing across Lakeview and into Mid-City, Carrollton, Gentilly, City Park and neighbourhoods farther south and east. Three major levees have now been breached

and 80 per cent of the city, an area the size of seven Manhattan Islands, is now under water. As night fell on a devastated region, the water was still rising in the city, and nobody was willing to predict when it would stop. After the destruction already apparent in the wake of Katrina, the American Red Cross was mobilising for what regional officials were calling the largest recovery operation in the organisation's history . . .

Terry Ebbert (*New Orleans Homeland Security Director*)

This is a national emergency. This is a national disgrace. FEMA has been here three days, yet there is no command and control. We can send massive amounts of aid to tsunami victims, but we can't bail out the city of New Orleans . . .

CNN Journalist

FEMA has been on the ground for four days, going into the fifth day. Why no massive airdrop of food and water? In Indonesia, they got food dropped two days after the tsunami struck . . .

NBC Journalist

Palettes of food and water have just been dropped at selected landing zones in the downtown area of New Orleans. It's an outrage because all of those elements existed before people died for lack of them: there was water, there was food, and there were choppers to drop both. Why no one was able to combine them in an airdrop is a cruel and criminal mystery of this dark chapter in our recent history. The concept of an airdrop of supplies was one we apparently introduced to the director of FEMA during a live interview on *Nightly News* on Thursday evening . . .

Governor Kathleen Blanco

God calls us to care for our fellow man, especially the neediest. I feel that call to lift up the less fortunate; the call to improve our communities and our state. It drives me to serve Louisiana as governor. I care for you. I want to make life safer and better for you . . .

We are seeing a show of force. It's putting confidence back in our hearts and in the minds of our people. These troops are battle-tested. They have M-16s and are locked and loaded. These troops know how to shoot and kill and I expect they will . . .

There is another fizzle and crackle as the electricity partially returns and the space is filled with more emergency lighting. The carnival float sits as if literally afloat in a large puddle. It is adorned by giant carnival heads, which include skulls. All around it is debris that can be utilised by the audience as seating, as well as tables and chairs from the ruined 'Funky Butt'. The audience members should be free to sit or stand as they see fit, and to adjust their position throughout if they like. The live action that follows is punctuated occasionally by further electrical explosions, collapsing structures, and rising water levels (all conveyed aurally).

There is musical intervention throughout; underscore, counterpoint, illustration, even echoes of the speech patterns of the actors. The aim is for music and sound to straddle and move between mimetic and diegetic worlds.

A tearful woman appears, and addresses the audience:

Beatrice

My name is Beatrice. My man Virgil, he had cancer, and I was nursing him in my apartment in the lower ninth ward. We had these oxygen canisters that kept him going, but when the hurricane came we ran out of air. He was suffocating, and I went out to see if there was anything I could find. I was halfway down the stairs before I knew I had to turn back. In the two minutes I was away he had died.

I called someone to ask what should I do with his body. They said take him across town to City Hall. Five miles of water between me and there, but that's what I did.

Beatrice *moves from the doorway and* **Virgil**'*s body appears in the form of a junk-puppet. He may well change shape and form throughout the piece, assisted by a growing collective of actors.*

Beatrice

Virgil wasn't no saint. He'd be out all night, drinking the bars dry. He liked his music, played the horn on Tipitina since he was a boy. Knew all those guys. He had kids all over the state, and he sure as hell wasn't faithful to me. But he was my man, and there was no way I was leavin' him to the rats and the water. So I wrapped him in the counterpane and I floated him all that way, and not a toe touched the water in all that time.

Slowly she guides the 'floating' corpse across the space as she speaks. She stops as **Miranda**, *carrying cans of food, emerges from another doorway and addresses* **Beatrice** *and the audience.*

Miranda

I was born out of wedlock. My dad was addicted to alcohol and my mom was addicted to him. I seen the hungry days. I seen the days with no lights and water in the house. I seen the days I couldn't find my mom or dad. I wouldn't wish my childhood on a dog.

Mama died, I was four, and her mother raised us. She was Choctaw Indian and she was hard. She was the kind of lady who'd file her fingernails on the sidewalk. But had it not been for that woman I don't know if we'd've made it.

Beatrice

Virgil and me, we weren't no kids. We'd been around. We knew a little 'bout dying, you hear? Verge, he lived hard 'cause he knew it wasn't gonna last. You hang tight, he said; hang tight, and let go light. And he did.

From here on it is assumed that **Beatrice** *continues to guide* **Virgil** *to City Hall. People emerge as she passes them, adding their voices to the collective and in turn helping her with* **Virgil***'s body. When not speaking, the cast acts very much as a Greek chorus, inhabiting whatever role needs to be filled; aside from* **Beatrice**, *characterisation is fluid. It perhaps goes without saying that the tenor is magic realist rather than naturalistic.*

Daniel *enters.*

Daniel

I'm Daniel – Dan, I prefer. I was wrongfully convicted of first-degree murder in '96. I was on death row for five years, in jail for ten, before the truth came out. The FBI had a report – they knew who killed the guy, and it wasn't me.

Since then I been job to job. It's real tough, 'cause no one wants to hear that you was innocent. All they know is that you were on death row.

Night before Katrina, the police pulled me in. No reason, just knew my name. So I'm in central lockup, and I'm like, this is a nightmare. I'm seeing death row again, everything is flashing back. I don't want to see this no more.

I used the phone, but there wasn't no one to call. I called my family. They was about to leave, they tried to find bail for me but they couldn't. They had to leave, so now I have to stay here and wait the storm out.

Here the music becomes a much more present feature, shaping **Miranda***'s speech.*

Miranda

I'm a singer. Music's what I do.

I was in my house when everything first started. When the hurricane came, it blew all the left side of my house off, and the water was coming in my house in torrents.

I had my neighbour, an elderly man, and myself, in the house with our dogs and cats, and we were trying to stay out of the water. But the water was coming in too fast. So we ended up having to leave the house.

We left the house and we went up on the roof of a school. I took a crowbar and I burst the door on the roof of the school to help people on the roof. Later on we found a flat boat, and we went around the neighbourhood getting people out of their houses and bringing them to the school.

The man that owns Wal-Mart got on the radio and he said to open the stores. My daughter went to see what she could get. At this point, it's survival. But while they were in the Wal-Mart the police came and started shooting in the place. And the police are shooting so they can get what *they* want. They were taking things back to the police station in their personal vehicles. You name it, they were stealing it and the residents were getting blamed for it.

We found all the food that we could and we cooked and we fed people. But then things started getting really bad.

Beatrice

As we travelled, Virgil and me, people came to help. We made him a raft out of a house door, and we laid him on it, safe and dry. Then we waded and swam, pushing him across the drowned city. Man, I'm glad he never saw what happened to this city. He loved New Orleans, and she loved him right back. And now she was weepin' for her man, like I was, and Verge he sailed on by and never once got wet.

Cal *passes, carrying a TV, only stopping on seeing* **Beatrice** *and the body.*

Cal

My name's Cal. My word's real. What I speak is real.

My mother died when I was nineteen. She had my kidney in a transplant and she died. Her body just rejected it. My kidney. I went crazy. I went crazy, man. That's how I've been living for a long time. Sometimes, man, I be kinda like welcoming death.

We're right there in the ninth ward during the storm, so we can see everything. We look out and we're like 'All right, well, shit, man, all this water rolling like this, there ain't nobody in those houses,' you know? So me and my Aunt T on the porch, and we're just like chillin', just lookin' at this hurricane, Katrina tearin' it up.

Next thing my Aunt T looked around, man, she said: 'Oh Lord Jesus! Oh Lord Jesus! Look at them two babies down in that water, Lord.'

So I look down and see the kids in the water, they was hollerin' 'Help!' So I pulled off my shirt and jumped right in the water. Everything was haywire, man. And I don't know what I was thinking. If you know me, I'm a low-life motherfucker. I'm thinkin' about me and only me. But I saw them two babies, I just lost everything. I didn't think. I didn't care nothing about life or death or whatever. I just knew I had to go jump in and get them babies, man.

And it all went good. The kids was alright. And one, the girl, she was sayin', 'Oh my mama, down there, my mama, my mama,' Her mama and some others, they was caught in an attic, and one of them was pregnant. So I knew I was gonna have to find a boat.

Beatrice

Folk was just holed up in their houses, hunkerin' down and wallin' themselves in. Ain't much money in our part of New Orleans, but lots of people they own their properties. Worked all their lives for them. They aren't gonna be leavin' them now. Your house is your life in these parts.

Some churchmen said afterwards we deserved to be drowned. Well, if bein' poor, an' having no car, and protecting your house means you deserved to be drowned, hell yeah, we deserved it.

Cal

This lady on the corner, Miss Ruth, she had a little skiff in her yard, and we took it. All these motherfuckers in an attic, and we paddled two blocks, you know what I'm sayin', and put them in the boat and brought 'em back to my Aunt T's. She was takin' care of everyone, man.

So man, we went in the stores and shit. We did a little lootin'. At the start, I wasn't thinkin' about savin' nobody. I'm thinking about my pocket. But then I guess something else happened. Something else got in the way. I forgot about money. It was something bigger than that and brother, it felt good in me, you heard me?

I used to be a dirty motherfucker. I was in the city to see what I could get. But getting them people, man, it felt good. It brung out the beast in me. The power of the beast. A survivor, you dig? And this one time in my life – actually, the second time with my mother's transplant – it made me feel good to say I did something good, you heard me?

And me and my cousin, we probably got about forty people from out there, at least. My Aunt T, she said fifty. But I don't know, I think that may be exaggerating just a little bit.

Beatrice

The water wasn't too bad at first; you could wade, and there were streets only ankle deep. It was only long after the storm had passed to the east that the city started flooding for real. And then it was swim – swim or sink.

Daniel

Late, late, maybe four on Monday morning. Hard wind, very hard wind. Lights went out in the jail. I was on the top floor. They had these little portholes that you can look out, and see the rain, the wind blowing, and the water starting to rise.

It was early. You can see the water constantly rising. You gotta remember, we're stuck in these cells. Guys on the bottom level, man, they hollerin' and screamin' for guards to come. No one comes. Begging, pleading, breakin' windows, burnin' sheets and blankets, flagging them to get attention. And no one came to help them.

The water had gone from chest high to chin high. Guys was on the top bunk with their head stuck out the ceiling to get air. They couldn't hold their breath that long.

The lights done gone out, so we was in the dark, with the water constantly rising. One thing we had to do, now, was to break out. We wasn't tryin' to break out to get out of jail, we breakin' out to save our lives.

One guy got out. He used this mop-wringer and busted a hole in the cell wall. This wringer, it's thick plastic with steel rods through it. If you keep banging on something with this thing, it'll crack. We chiselled through the concrete to the next cell. It took hours, man. All the cells is next to each other, so you gotta knock holes in each one and meantime some guy was working on the door, just kickin' away. If your ankles don't break, you be alright.

The guys at the bottom were just hollerin' and screamin'. The police had left. They scared to death, and some we couldn't get out. The rest of us got out Monday night.

When we finally got out, that's where the guards were sitting at, outside. They were sitting on their boats. Just sitting there, waiting. They know we were getting out. About a thousand guys escaped, and they just put us on boats and took us to Broad Street, to the bridge, and put us there.

Miranda

By the second day, with the people that were there, that we were feeding and everything, we had no more food and no water. We had nothing, and other people were coming in our neighbourhood. We were watching the helicopters going and airlifting other people out, but they would hover over us and tell us 'Hi!' and that would be all. They wouldn't drop us any food or any water, or nothing.

The Mayor had told everyone to leave, but most folk in New Orleans don't own cars and there ain't no buses, so how we going to leave? Plus, for those folk on welfare, the end of the month meant no cash, so how they going to survive out of the city with just the clothes on their back?

So we went to the Superdome first, like the Mayor said. It's amazing how in a powerful city like New Orleans, they just going to have one place, the Superdome. How are they going to fill the whole entire city of New Orleans in the Superdome? The ceiling tiles was falling on people, on their heads. It was smoking real bad in there, a fire all the way to the top. Everybody in the dome was mad, it was downtown Baghdad in there.

Beatrice

We sailed right on by the Superdome. Man, ain't no way we be goin' there, we could hear the yellin' two blocks back. It was a circle of hell in there, you know, and I sure didn't feel like joinin'. I ain't disrespectin' Verge further by stretching him out in no Superdome. City Hall was the only way for us.

Cal

It was Tuesday. I went to Gentilly. It was hectic, man, everything was going on – lootin' robbin', jackin'. Man, all kinds of stuff. Brothers walkin around with Uzis and shit. It was off the chain over there, you dig?

I knew a lot of cats. So I'm over there, doin' my thing, whatever I do. I ain't even gonna go into that here. That's another chapter. Anyway, I'm doin' my thing and it got kinda dark, and I knew I had to make it home. But I also knew I had two miles of water in front of me.

So I grabbed a piece of board and I stroked all the way home. Now, I heard brothers say they done got bit by something, something that snatched their leg and took them underwater. I actually saw 'em in hospital with teeth marks, where one dude got bit. But I stroked all the way home on that board, and nothing touched me. I didn't run into no obstacles, just looked at the stars and never touched nothin'.

I tell you, I got some weird shit that happened in my life. But I guess God was with me. When I came for the hurricane I had the wrong things on my mind. I was an opportunist. At least I thought I was.

Miranda

The Superdome was too much. As soon as we saw what was going on there, me and my Gaynell, my daughter, we left. Some others came with us too and we started walking and wading and struggling through again. We heard alligators had come in from the Mississippi, and they were eating people. They had all kinds of stuff in the water. They had babies floating in the water.

We had to walk over bodies of dead people. People that we tried to save from the hospices, from the hospitals and from the old folks' homes. I tried to get the police to help us, but

I realised they were in the same situation we were. We rescued some police officers in the flat boat from the Fifth District police station. The guy who was in the boat, he rescued a lot of them and brought them to different places so they could be saved.

We understood that the police couldn't help us, but we couldn't understand why the National Guard and them couldn't help us, because we kept seeing them but they never would stop and help us.

Beatrice

Virgil and me, we kept clear of the police. They weren't what you'd call friendly to us when the city was dry, ain't no reason to think they'd be helpful now all hell was loose. We saw 'em, though. Saw 'em ignore folk. Saw 'em offer to help one white girl if she showed 'em her titties. Saw 'em make things worse.

Larry *and* **Lorrie** *enter together, also from the audience. Initially they stay on the fringes of the audience, only later helping* **Beatrice** *and* **Virgil***'s krewe.*

Larry

On day two, there were approximately five hundred of us tourists left in the hotels in the French Quarter. Some of us had cellphone contact with family and friends outside of New Orleans. We were repeatedly told that all sorts of resources including the National Guard and scores of buses were pouring into the city. The buses and the other resources must have been invisible because none of us had seen them.

Lorrie

By day four our hotels had run out of fuel and water. Sanitation was abysmal. As the desperation and despair increased, street crime as well as water levels began to rise. The hotels turned us out and locked their doors, telling us that the 'officials' told us to report to the Convention Centre to wait for more buses. As we entered the centre of the city we finally encountered the National Guard.

Larry

The Guards told us we would not be allowed into the Superdome as the City's primary shelter had descended into a humanitarian and health hellhole. The guards also told us that the only other shelter, the Convention Centre, was also descending into chaos and squalor and that the police were not allowing anyone else in. We asked, 'If we can't go to the only two shelters in the city, what is our alternative?' The Guards told us that that was our problem, and no, they did not have extra water to give to us.

Lorrie

We walked to the police command centre on Canal Street and were told the same thing, that we were on our own, and no, they did not have water to give us. We now numbered several hundred. We held a mass meeting to decide a course of action. We agreed to camp outside the police command post. We would be plainly visible to the media and would constitute a visible embarrassment to the city officials. The police told us that we could not stay. Regardless, we began to settle in and set up camp. In short order, the police commander came across the street to address our group. He told us he had a solution: we should walk to the Pontchartrain Expressway and cross the greater New Orleans Bridge where the police had buses lined up to take us out of the city. The crowed cheered and began to move. We called everyone back and explained to the commander that there had been lots of misinformation and was he sure that there were buses waiting for us. The commander turned to the crowd and stated emphatically, 'I swear to you that the buses are there.'

Larry

We organised ourselves and the two hundred of us set off for the bridge. As we marched past the Convention Centre,

many locals saw our group and asked where we were headed. We told them about the great news. Families immediately grabbed their few belongings and quickly our numbers doubled and then doubled again. Babies in strollers now joined us, people using crutches, elderly clasping walkers and others in wheelchairs. We marched the two or three miles to the freeway and up the steep incline to the bridge. It now began to pour down rain.

Daniel

I was on the Broad Street Bridge from Monday night until Thursday with nothing to eat, nothing to drink. But the guards, they had water and they wouldn't give us a cup. They was taunting us, giving it to their dogs in front of us. Majority of them white. I don't look at colour, I'm not racist, I look at status. If you poor, it don't matter if you white or black, you get mistreated in Louisiana. If you don't have nothin' we all in the same boat.

Beatrice

All along the way, people saw us and came to help. They gave me a little food, some juice – orange and pomegranate it was. They fixed the raft now and again, 'cause it was made in a rush and I ain't no shipbuilder, you know? There was times the road was blocked and we had to go round, or go through houses to the next street. But no one minded us goin' through, and sometimes we rested in the houses and got our breath.

Daniel

For four days you can't move. You had guys defecating on themselves, urinating on themselves. You couldn't move. Guys getting diabetic comas, seizures, heat strokes. It was a nightmare. You had guys drinking the filthy flood water. They shootin', spraying mace on everybody. It's random.

I'm thinking we gonna die on this bridge, either from starvation or dehydration. No one cares. These people is gonna go on a killing spree and kill everyone on this bridge. They was looking for a reason to shoot someone. They had guns. They had assault rifles. They had the right equipment if they want to slaughter us. They had the right equipment.

Cal

New Orleans is politically run by fucked-up ass-mentality police officers. Motherfuckers just as human as me, but they got a badge. They're in Wal-Mart, stealin'. Pathetic. Of all places, Wal-Mart. Goddam. They at least try a bank or something, you know what I'm sayin'? You got on a blue uniform, you can go anywhere. If I was police and I was stealin', it wouldn't be Wal-Mart. It's a lack of imagination. That's my point.

Miranda

I had two other sisters the other side of the Mississippi River Bridge. They told me, 'You just try to get to us, the lights are on over here.' So we attempted to cross the bridge, and this where we met with the resistance. The police told us to turn around or risk being shot. The police told us this. Guns raised. 'Turn around or get shot.'

They had police all over the place, military all over the place, FEMA all over the place. And nobody was doing anything to help us. It was just blatant. They boxed us in that city. They said if we tried to get out, they'd shoot to kill. And let me tell you something: that's nothing new for New Orleans.

Lorrie

As we approached the bridge, armed Gretna sheriffs formed a line across the foot of the bridge. Before we were close enough to speak, they began firing their weapons over our heads.

We hear this from behind the audience

This sent the crowd fleeing in various directions. As the crowd scattered and dissipated, a few of us inched forward and managed to engage some of the sheriffs in conversation. We told them of our conversation with the police commander and of the commander's assurances. The sheriffs informed us there were no buses waiting. The commander had lied to us to get us to move.

We asked why we couldn't cross the bridge anyway, especially as there was little traffic on the six-lane highway. They responded that the West Bank was not going to become New Orleans and there would be no Superdomes in their city.

Larry

We retreated back down Highway 90 to seek shelter from the rain under an overpass. We debated our options and in the end decided to build an encampment in the middle of the Ponchartrain Expressway on the centre divide. We would be visible to everyone, we would have some security being on an elevated freeway and we could wait and watch for the arrival of the yet-to-be-seen buses.

Beatrice

Boats would pass, occasionally, but no one was interested in the dead. They was lookin' for the livin', those that still breathed, and at that moment that was fair enough.
I didn't wanna share Virgil with no one just then, even if we did get there quicker.

Sometime it felt we were goin' round in circles. We started right there in the Ninth, and sometimes it seemed we never got too far away from our old neighbourhood. Virgil, he didn't want to leave, not yet, not without takin' one last look at the places he loved.

He nearly died once before. Can't live like Verge did and not hit trouble once a while. Comin' home late one night he took a detour through some woman's bedroom. Turns out there was a contract of marriage pressin', you know what I'm saying? Virgil he was out the window double time, but he wasn't as young as he used to be and her man was faster. Three weeks in hospital, a punctured lung and perforated ears he got for that one. From that point on his hearing started to go. Took a few years, but in time it got so he'd say it was like listenin' underwater.

We hear this, as from **Virgil***'s perspective, the rest of* **Beatrice***'s speech muffled in just this fashion.*

To make sense of stuff he had to check in with his body first – that was his tuning fork, everythin' started and finished there, like the world was in his head. He'd play by sight and by touch. 'Bee, I can still feel, girl,' he'd say. 'I got the beat running over my skin like water, and that bass I can feel like a topcoat. (*Touches his shoulders.*) An' her (*indicates Miranda*) voice, it's like I see it, like a blue-green light shinin' on my soul. So don't you be worryin' Bee – only thing I can't hear is the price of liquor!'

All this has been audible as if we're in his head. Gradually it returns to normal for **Daniel'***s speech.*

Daniel

They put us all on buses Thursday and took us to Hunt Correctional Centre. We think we gonna get water, food. And it only gets worse.

It was a prison football field. Twelve hundred guys on the ground. And Louisiana's made out of swampland, so it's wet, you got gnats, you got mosquitoes. It's like you're a wild animal in a cage. I saw stabbings. Guys would go around jacking guys' blankets from them, beating them up. Gangs were formed. It was worse than the bridge.

Miranda

So me and Gaynell, we thought OK, now where do we go? And we heard people were heading for the Convention Centre. Now I wasn't sure. I'd seen the Superdome and I figured it would be a miracle for the Centre to be safe. But Gaynell, she wanted to go; her little baby was tired and we'd walked so far. So we went.

We arrived, and there wasn't even room inside. We had to stay by the door, on the sidewalk, with everyone else. Only benefit was it was dry.

Beatrice

He was married, you know. And not to me. His wife was over in Baton Rouge and I was here. She wasn't too comfortable with the arrangement but I was cool. With Virgil, you knew going in what the scene was, or if you didn't you was blind. You knew the situation, and you danced with it or you sat it out, but wasn't no point tryin' to change the music. It was what it was. And the man was kind, you know? When he was here it was all about me and him. He'd have his stories and his dreams of the future – you know, build a home, settle down – but it was all bullshit and he knew it. Just helped pretend he was the same as everyone else. Well, now the stories are over, and this is how it is. Just me and this body, floating through a city of the dead.

Miranda

Well, I had got tired using the restroom on the sidewalk, so I crept into the Convention Centre to use the restroom there.

What I seen when I came out I will remember for the rest of my life. I swear, God be my judge. I'm crouched trying to get back to the kids. I see everyone on the street. Everyone is sitting on the ground with their hands in the air. The cops are stationed in different spots, with their guns aimed at people. I look at my five-year-old granddaughter, Ariel, and the light from one of the guns was actually on her forehead.

My oldest daughter, Gaynell, she's like, you want to go ballistic when you see someone do something like this to your child but you can't do nothing because you both might get killed. Ariel is sitting with her hands in the air. And she's past afraid, she's terrified. And she's asking her mama, Gaynell, 'Am I doing it right?' because even the babies know the police kill in New Orleans. So she's asking her mama: 'Am I doing it right? Am I doing it right?'

Lorrie

All day long, we saw other families, individuals and groups make the same trip up the incline in an attempt to cross the bridge, only to be turned away. Some chased away with gunfire, others simply told no, others to be verbally berated and humiliated. Thousands of New Orleaners were prevented and prohibited from self-evacuating the city on foot. The only way across the bridge was by vehicle. We saw workers stealing trucks, buses, moving vans, semi-trucks and any car that could be hot-wired.

Miranda

Finally it got to be too much, I just took all of the people that I could from outside the Convention Centre. I had two old women in wheelchairs with no legs, that I rowed them from down there in that nightmare to the French Quarter, and I went back and got more people.

There were groups of us, there were about twenty-four of us, and we kept going back and forth and rescuing whoever we could get and bringing them to the French Quarter because we heard that there were phones in the French Quarter, and that there wasn't any water. And they were right, there were phones, but we couldn't get through to anyone.

Beatrice

More and more now we was getting buzzed by helicopters. Some news, I guess, and some police. Virgil was a big white signal on the black water, and they came like flies to flowers. But none of them tried to pick us up. We was just a story to them, that's all. So they buzzed and they blew the water into a frenzy and they made it hard to keep Virgil afloat, but they never helped.

One time I was tryin' so hard to keep my man afloat I done lost my glasses. Weren't much use anyhow, in all that water, but you're used to seeing things a certain way, you know? Now I ain't blind, but I can't see too well either, and I felt kinda naked without them. So I was tryin' to get close to things, to hear how we was movin'. And once the storm stopped, it was eerie quiet sometimes with no cars or conversation. So I listened to the sound bounce off the houses, and I listened to where the choppers seemed to be comin' from, and I got close to street signs when I could. It was like I became a part of everythin' else; the more I forgot about me, the better I got around. Like I was an echo myself.

All this again we hear; the next few of **Beatrice***'s accounts have this sonic puppetry accompanying them.*

Lorrie

Our little camp began to blossom. Someone stole a water delivery truck and brought it up to us. A mile or so down the freeway, an army truck lost a couple of pallets of C-rations on a tight turn. We ferried the food back to our camp in shopping carts. With food and water, co-operation, community and creativity flowered. We organised a clean up and hung garbage bags from the rebar poles. We made beds from wood pallets and cardboard. We designated a storm drain as the bathroom and the kids built an elaborate enclosure for privacy out of plastic, broken umbrellas and other scraps. We even organised a food recycling system where individuals could swap out parts of C-rations – apple sauce for babies and candies for kids.

Larry

This was a process we saw repeatedly in the aftermath of Katrina. When individuals had to fight to find food or water, it meant looking out for yourself only. You had to do whatever it took to find water for your kids or food for your parents. When these basic needs were met, people began to look out for each other, working together and constructing a community. If the relief organisations had saturated the City with food and water in the first two or three days, the desperation, the frustration and the ugliness would not have set in.

Cal

Friday, the water level's slowly dropping. We look around; the house is trashed. I mean totally destroyed – it's like *Titanic*. Ain't nothing left worth saving. So we push off for the last time. My aunt's wailing, arms wavin'. Man, she grew up in that house. Nothing left at all. And later, we find she ain't covered. Oh, she got hurricane insurance all right, but the company man says it was the flood, not the wind. Now, I done some shit in my life, ain't pleading no excuses, but you tell me: you in insurance? How the fuck do you live with yourself? Seriously. You in politics, yeah? I got a gun. Put it in your mouth, pull the trigger, do the world a favour.

Beatrice

After a time the helicopters got bored and left us alone. I guess we was old news. Seemed somehow Virgil was enjoying the fuss – always did like to be the centre of attention, you know? Was like a new world opened up to me now the city was turned upside down, now my ears was unlocked. As we travelled I got such a sense that he was still with me, now I was really listenin', not only his body but something else. Like his spirit wasn't going to leave till we got where we was goin'. I wasn't leading, I was following, you know? Even though I couldn't see who or what was ahead. I wasn't alone, that's for sure.

Lorrie

We offered food and water to passing families and individuals. Many decided to stay and join us. Our encampment grew to eighty or ninety people. From a woman with a battery-powered radio we learned that the media was talking about us. Up in full view on the freeway, every relief and news organisation saw us on their way into the city. Officials were being asked what they were going to do about all those families living up on the freeway? The officials responded they were going to take care of us. Some of us got a sinking feeling. 'Taking care of us' had an ominous tone to it.

Beatrice

Virgil, he was always journeyin'. Never in the same place for long. He'd skip on in and see the view, see the scene, then skip on out again. I guess he was restless, always got an itch, never know where home was. One time he was over in Baton Rouge and his daddy died. Took two days for the word to reach him from out there in the hills where his folks lived. Well, he made it back for the funeral by the skin of it, but man, he was gone before the party was over, playin' the horn somewhere out of state or just cuttin' loose. Always slidin', always rollin'. Everyone knew Virgil, but no one for more than five minutes. He went off like a firework in their lives and then he was gone till the next time.

Miranda

Saturday is when we finally got on a bus. They sent us all to College Station, to a Methodist church. One of these ladies' husbands had some real estate, and he just gave us the keys to one of his houses without any money. God bless this man. He gave us keys and told us to get back in touch once we got the FEMA money. He gave us time.

All through, I'm thinking: how could it be? How could it be that a country which is supposedly the richest country in the world, where the 82nd Airborne are prepared to be anywhere in the world in a day and a half, where we were in Sri Lanka when the tsunami hit in less than two days, yet here we are, day four, day five, and the Federal government still has not made it to New Orleans? Don't we deserve a home? Somewhere to live? Whatever happened to American hospitality?

Respect the state, they say. Allegiance to the flag, they say. But what is the state but the people? What does the flag symbolise but the people? What kind of organisation only protects the rich, only cares for those who pay it the most? I tell you what; the Mob, that's what. Now, you tell me how this ain't just one big protection racket, you hear?

Daniel

They took us from the field to Alexandria, where we finally got fed. I was there a month, and they found out who I was, calling me nigger, killer, death-row killer. I was sent to the hole. They thought I was still on death row.

Larry

Unfortunately, our sinking feeling was correct. Just as dusk set in, a Gretna sheriff showed up, jumped out of his patrol vehicle, aimed his gun at our faces, screaming, 'Get off the fucking freeway.' A helicopter arrived and used the wind from its blades to blow away our flimsy structures. As we retreated, the sheriff loaded up his truck with our food and water.

Lorrie

In the pandemonium of having our camp raided and destroyed, we scattered once again. Reduced to a small group of eight people, in the dark, we sought refuge in an abandoned school bus, under the freeway on Cilo Street. We were hiding from possible criminal elements but equally and definitely we were hiding from the police and sheriffs with their martial law, curfew and shoot-to-kill policies.

Beatrice

I couldn't do it all at once. I had to rest, to sleep. So Virgil he brought me to a big ol' place by the river, the Melpomene pump station it was, though no one was there doing any pumpin', and we found a platform high up to stretch out and sleep on. Place was dark as hell, but I'd been without my glasses for so long now it made no difference. I just felt my way around. Verge, he'd always say to feel the sound, not to hear it, so that's what I done. And we went up higher and higher, till we found our safety. And we took our rest.

Daniel

From Hunt we were in Alexandria for thirty days, in the hole and then in a cell. And then I finally got lucky. This attorney came with a human rights group, and that backed the guards off us to start with. And these lawyers knew my name, from my time on death row, and they acted fast. They got in touch with my lawyers from way back, Clive Stafford-Smith and Ben Cohen, and we went to court. This little hick court, kangeroo court, twenty guards in the courtroom. Ain't nowhere in the country you find guards in the courtroom, 'cept here. And Ben gave them an ultimatum, filed a writ of habeas corpus and produced our bodies in court, 'cause you know, misdemeanours don't carry no more than thirty days for the charges I had. It was that fast: we was seen, and then these guys went into action. So they cut all misdemeanours, cut us loose and brought us to these shelters.

Miranda

When I finally did get back to the ninth ward, and not just in my neighbourhood, but in other neighbourhoods in the ninth ward, there were a lot of people still trapped down there. Old people, young people, babies, pregnant women. I mean, nobody was helping them.

But what I want people to understand is that, if we hadn't been left down there like the animals that they were treating us like, all of those things wouldn't have happened. People are trying to say that we stayed in that city because we wanted to be rioting and we wanted to do this and we didn't have resources to get out, we had no way to leave. When they gave the evacuation order, if we could've left, we would have left.

And I want people to realise that we did not stay in the city so we could steal and loot and commit crimes. A lot of those young men lost their minds because the helicopters would fly over us and they wouldn't stop. We would make SOS on the flashlights, we'd do everything, and it really did come to a point where these young men were so frustrated that they did start shooting. They weren't trying to hit the helicopters, they figured maybe they weren't seeing. Maybe if they hear this gunfire they will stop then. But that didn't help us. Nothing like that helped us.

I don't want them arresting nobody. I broke the window in an RTA bus. I never learned how to drive a bus in my life. I got in that bus. I loaded all of those people in wheelchairs and in everything else into that bus, and we drove and we drove and we drove and millions of people was trying to get me to help them to get on the bus, too.

Beatrice

I woke up to find the Melpomene had flooded overnight. We was dry, high up by the roof, but we was trapped. So I sat and listened to the water rise, thinking, 'Well, Verge, I'm with you soon, boy.' And I sang a little bit, sang one of Virgil's tragic old songs. But then I was lookin' round, lookin' up, I guess to God above, and I see a patch of light. My eyes weren't up to much, but they could still do light; it was like all was still night but a window of heaven had opened above and I felt heat on my face.

A spotlight illustrates this.

I see a skylight and part of the roof's been broken off by the storm. So we wait for the water to reach us and then we push off again, me in the water, treadin' water, and Virgil on the old door. And the flood, it took us right up to the roof, and through that hole.

So Virgil, he looked after me still. On the roof we could see City Hall, a few blocks away, and it looked dry.

Under the next speech **Virgil** *and* **Beatrice** *are hauled up the face of the float, across the face of the largest head, to safety.*

Lorrie

The next days, our group of eight walked most of the day, made contact with New Orleans Fire Department and were eventually airlifted out by an urban search-and-rescue team. We were dropped off near the airport and managed to catch a ride with the National Guard. The two young guardsmen apologised for the limited response of the Louisiana Guards. They explained that a large section of their unit was in Iraq and that meant they were short-handed and were unable to complete all the tasks they were assigned.

We arrived at the airport on the day a massive airlift had begun. The airport had become another Superdome. We were caught in a press of humanity as flights were delayed for several hours while George Bush landed briefly at the airport for a photo op. After being evacuated on a coastguard cargo plane, we arrived in San Antonio, Texas.

Cal

Look how the city looks. Look. This shit kills me. Look at Nagin sayin' like it's all good. Dude's phony, man. What a joke. On national television, talking 'bout getting the casinos started. It's all about the money, baby. It's all about the Benjamins. 'Come back, eat the gumbo.' Shit.

How can a police superintendent get a two-million-dollar book deal to write about the tragedy of Katrina? Was he there? He wasn't in it when it was the grind, bro. I'm the one should be getting' paid. I'm the one drinking that motherfucking water, haulin' them people out. We was in it, knee deep, you heard me? I was coming for the wrong things and I still didn't end up making no money, man. I ended up helping people, and that was cool.

Beatrice (*from the top of the float*)
Virgil and me, we made it up there. We got to City Hall. And the place was one long stretch of bodies, like after a war. Under tarps, under blankets; grievin' families all around, frozen like they was statues in a cemetery or some sort of parade, paused like on a video. So we joined them, sat ourselves down, and we waited. And this time when they eventually came to take Virgil away, I did not look back.

She exits.

Daniel
New Orleans is where my history lies. It's like, you can't go nowhere and see another Bourbon Street. And that's why I'm so tied to New Orleans. And I figure, if I'm not doing anything illegal, why would I keep havin' to run and hide? So, that's the thing with me and New Orleans.

Cal
After we got out of New Orleans we lived out of a microwave for two months in Dallas, but that's cool because it's half the battle when you're doing it with family. I never had a father but I love my kids, man.

Motherfucker means to be there but it's so rough. Mainly financially. I feel like if a motherfucker had some money, a motherfucker'd be straight. I don't care if you live in Cairo, Egypt, if I got some money I'll come see you. You ain't got no money, you can't make no move. It's rough, man. Gotta keep your head above water, though.

If I can get twenty more years out of this body, I want it. I'm gonna squeeze every piece of life I can squeeze out of it. I know how important that is now. I do. I ain't never in my life thought about smelling flowers. I smelled the flowers. I know what life is, now. Never know till it is all gone, twinkle of an eye, bro. Twinkle of an eye, it can all be gone, just like that. You'll be like your boy in *Ghost*, then, Patrick Swayze. Trying to find your way home, you heard me? Tryin' to find your way home.

The lights go down on everything else. The cast now have all left, with **Virgil***'s body.*

Storey Three

PART TWO

Koppel and Brown's interview is relayed aurally and can be heard on the stairwell to floor four as well as throughout the rooms on floor three.

Ted Koppel (*anchorman, ABC* Nightline)
Earlier this evening I spoke with Mike Brown, the director of the Federal Emergency Management Agency, he's co-ordinating disaster relief of a dozen Federal agencies and the American Red Cross. I asked about the discrepancy between FEMA's estimate of the number of people at the Convention Centre and the Mayor's estimate.

Michael Brown (*FEMA Director*)
Actually, I have sent General Honore of the First Army to find out exactly the truth of what's down there because we first learned of the Convention Centre, we – we being the Federal government – today.

Ted Koppel
I've heard you say during the course of this evening on a number of interviews you just found out about it today. This is the fifth day. Don't you guys watch television? Don't you guys listen to the radio? Our reporters have been reporting about it for more than just today.

Michael Brown
We learned about it factually today that, that what existed. We've been so focused on doing rescue and life-saving missions and evacuating people from the Superdome that when we first learned about it, of course, my first gut instinction, instinct was, get somebody in there, get me truth on the ground, let me know, because if it's true we've got to help those people. And I want to say to the American people that they do need to understand exactly how catastrophic this disaster is, and they do need to know that

we're gonna have every available resource to do everything that we can. We're gonna take care of these victims, we're gonna make it right. We're gonna make certain, we're gonna make absolutely certain that the devastation that has been reaped upon these people is taken care of and that we get their lives back in order.

Ted Koppel

Mr Brown, some of these people are dead. They're beyond your help. Some of these people that have died because they needed insulin and they couldn't get it. Some of the people died because they were in hospitals and they couldn't get the assistance that they needed. You say you were surprised by the fact that so many people didn't make it out. It's no surprise to anyone that you had at least a hundred thousand people in the city of New Orleans who are dirt poor. Who don't have cars, who don't have access to public transportation, who don't have any way of getting out of the city simply because somebody says, 'You know, there's a force-five storm coming, you ought to get out.' If you didn't have buses there to get them out, why should it be a surprise to you that they stayed?

Michael Brown

Well, Ted, you know, we're, I'm not going to sit here and second-guess – why or when evacuation orders were given or why or why not the city didn't have buses available. And I don't make judgments about why people choose not to evacuate. But you know, there was a mandatory evacuation of New Orleans. And to find people still there is just heart-wrenching to me because the Mayor did everything he could to get them out of there. I think the death toll may go into the thousands. And unfortunately, that's going to be attributable, a lot to people who did not heed the evacuation warnings. No disaster is perfect. Mistakes are made in every single disaster.

Now, I'm going to go home and walk my dog and hug my wife, and maybe get a good Mexican meal and a stiff margarita and a full night's sleep. And then I'm going to go right back to FEMA and continue to do all I can to help these victims.

The audience is ushered back out of the bar and through the adjacent rooms; these are similarly wrecked versions of the ones encountered below. The shotgun house has become a kind of shrine to its lost former owners. At the rear another flight of stairs takes everyone to the final floor: the interior of an old New Orleans church. The audience fill the space, which runs the length of the building, sitting or standing as they see fit.

Storey Four

FUNERAL

To music a coffin is borne in: **Virgil***'s. The cast, now all in white, follow and process it to the grave, which is revealed to be in the middle of the audience; the spectators, therefore, automatically become mourners at a funeral, their own black waterproofs acting as mourning gear. This should be slow and mesmerising, the actors stepping in New Orleans funeral style, accompanied by Charlie Miller's 'Prayer for New Orleans' and other such weird and lamenting music.*

The burial itself is extremely emotional, accompanied by wailing from the women and a fervent sermon from the **Preacher***. The audience should be included at all times.*

Preacher

My text today is taken from a great preacher of the past; one of the greatest, indeed, a man who knew a thing or two about loss, and about bad leaders.

'If we understood aright the dignity of this bell that tolls for our evening prayer, we would be glad to make it ours. The bell doth toll for him that thinks it doth; and from that minute that that occasion wrought upon him, he is united to God. Who casts not up his eye to the sun when it rises? Who takes off his eye from a comet when that breaks out? Who bends not his ear to any bell, which upon any occasion rings? But who can remove it from that bell, which is passing a piece of himself out of this world? No man is an island, entire of itself; every man is a piece of the continent, a part of the main; if a clod be washed away by the sea, Europe is the less, as well as if a promontory were, as well as if a manor of thy friends or of thine own were; any man's death diminishes me, because I am involved in mankind. And therefore never send to know for whom the bell tolls. It tolls for thee. Amen.'

Beatrice *steps forward and sings. She finishes, and there is a second line from the trombone and a cry from the cast and the occasion immediately becomes a rather riotous celebration.*

On the exit walls the following quotation is scrawled:

Screw this! They're lying! The President's lying! The rich fat cats that are drowning you will do it again and again and again. They lead you into imperialist wars for profit, they take away your schools and your hope and when you complain, they blame Blacks and Jews and immigrants. Then they push your kids under. I say, kick'm in the ass and take your rightful share!

HUEY LONG, *Governor of Louisiana (1927)*

There then follows a raucous cacophony of recorded sound: music (blues and jazz from 1927 etc.), testimony (Bushes, West, Nagin, Brown, etc.), other text (including Genesis and Congressional hearings) and so forth. The lights dim to black, the sound crescendoes, and then abruptly everything stops.

The audience exits via a different doorway to that through which they entered. Above it is ivory.

Methuen Drama Student Editions

Jean Anouilh *Antigone* • John Arden *Serjeant Musgrave's Dance* Alan Ayckbourn *Confusions* • Aphra Behn *The Rover* • Edward Bond *Lear* • *Saved* • Bertolt Brecht *The Caucasian Chalk Circle* • *Fear and Misery in the Third Reich* • *The Good Person of Szechwan* • *Life of Galileo* • *Mother Courage and her Children* • *The Resistible Rise of Arturo Ui* • *The Threepenny Opera* • Anton Chekhov *The Cherry Orchard* • *The Seagull* • *Three Sisters* • *Uncle Vanya* • Caryl Churchill *Serious Money* • *Top Girls* • Shelagh Delaney *A Taste of Honey* • Euripides *Elektra* • *Medea* • Dario Fo *Accidental Death of an Anarchist* • Michael Frayn *Copenhagen* • John Galsworthy *Strife* • Nikolai Gogol *The Government Inspector* • Robert Holman *Across Oka* • Henrik Ibsen *A Doll's House* • *Ghosts* • *Hedda Gabler* • Charlotte Keatley *My Mother Said I Never Should* • Bernard Kops *Dreams of Anne Frank* • Federico García Lorca *Blood Wedding* • *Doña Rosita the Spinster* (bilingual edition) • *The House of Bernarda Alba* • (bilingual edition) • *Yerma* (bilingual edition) • David Mamet *Glengarry Glen Ross* • *Oleanna* • Patrick Marber *Closer* • John Marston *Malcontent* • Martin McDonagh *The Lieutenant of Inishmore* • Joe Orton *Loot* • Luigi Pirandello *Six Characters in Search of an Author* • Mark Ravenhill *Shopping and F***ing* • Willy Russell *Blood Brothers* • *Educating Rita* • Sophocles *Antigone* • *Oedipus the King* • Wole Soyinka *Death and the King's Horseman* • Shelagh Stephenson *The Memory of Water* • August Strindberg *Miss Julie* • J. M. Synge *The Playboy of the Western World* • Theatre Workshop *Oh What a Lovely War* Timberlake Wertenbaker *Our Country's Good* • Arnold Wesker *The Merchant* • Oscar Wilde *The Importance of Being Earnest* • Tennessee Williams *A Streetcar Named Desire* • *The Glass Menagerie*